Wildfires

Kathy Furgang

NATIONAL GEOGRAPHIC

Washington, D.C.

For Mom —K. F.

Trade paperback ISBN: 978-1-4263-2133-7
Reinforced library binding ISBN: 978-1-4263-2134-4

Editor: Shelby Alinsky
Art Director: Amanda Larsen
Editorial: Snapdragon Books
Designer: YAY! Design
Photo Editor: Lori Epstein
Rights Clearance Specialist: Michael Cassady
Manufacturing Manager: Rachel Faulise
Production Assistants: Sanjida Rashid and Rachel Kenny

The author and publisher gratefully acknowledge the expert content review of this book by Ilana Abrahamson of the University of Montana's FireCenter and the U.S. Forest Service's Missoula Fire Sciences Laboratory, and the literacy review of this book by Mariam Jean Dreher, professor of reading education at the University of Maryland, College Park.

Illustration Credits

National Geographic supports K–12 educators with ELA Common Core Resources.
Visit natgeoed.org/commoncore for more information.

Printed in the United States of America
15/WOR/1

Table of Contents

Fire!

Yellowstone National Park, in Wyoming, U.S.A., is a popular vacation spot. But in the summer of 1988, it was a danger to the public. Why? The place visited for its beautiful scenery was going up in smoke!

The expression "spread like wildfire" comes from the fact that wildfires can grow very quickly, like the ones in Yellowstone National Park in the summer of 1988.

Hot Word

WILDFIRE: an uncontrolled fire that occurs outdoors, especially over a wooded area

The wildfires started slowly. But then they picked up speed. The park soon closed to the public. Fires burned for nearly four months. By the end, almost one million acres of the park had burned.

Gigantic wildfires like the ones in Yellowstone don't happen very often. But they *are* common in wilderness areas. Some can get very large and spread quickly. They can put people and property in danger. Other fires stay small, before going out on their own.

Wildfires stretch across the hills of San Diego County, California, U.S.A., threatening to burn a nearby house.

After a fire, plants grow back and animals return. In fact, wildfires are an important part of nature.

An area that burned in a wildfire can quickly see new plant growth.

Up in Smoke

Even the biggest wildfire starts with a single spark. A lightning strike is a common way for a fire to ignite. Volcanoes can also start fires when hot lava ignites grass or brush. Other wildfires start when people are careless with matches or when building campfires.

Hot Word

IGNITE: to catch fire

Lightning strikes Earth more than 100,000 times a day.

A wildfire needs three things in order to burn: heat, fuel, and oxygen.

A source of **heat** starts a fire and keeps it going. Heat might come from a lightning strike or a match.

Fuel gives a fire the energy it needs to keep burning. Fuel can be trees, other plants, or fallen leaves.

Fires also need **oxygen.** For fuel to burn, it must react with oxygen in the air.

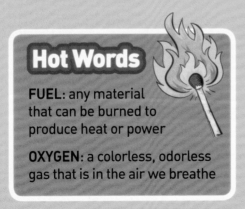

Hot Words

FUEL: any material that can be burned to produce heat or power

OXYGEN: a colorless, odorless gas that is in the air we breathe

This combination of heat, fuel, and oxygen is called the fire triangle. A fire can be put out by removing any part of the triangle.

Wildfires can burn in three different ways.

ground fire

A ground fire is a slow-moving fire. It burns dead, rotting leaves and the roots of plants on or in the ground.

A surface fire moves along the forest floor from plant to plant. It also burns fallen leaves and branches.

surface fire

A crown fire spreads quickly in the tops of trees. Winds can cause a crown fire to change direction in an instant.

All three types of fire can happen in the same wildfire.

crown fire

Weird but true!

A wildfire can move as fast as 14 miles an hour.

13

Wildfires can happen almost anywhere in the world. But they happen most often in places with hot, dry weather. In these conditions, a spark can quickly ignite a fire.

In the fall in southern California, U.S.A., the Santa Ana winds blow dry air from the desert over the mountains. Once a wildfire starts, these winds make the fire grow fast.

This satellite image shows several wildfires burning in southern California. The Santa Ana winds fan the flames and blow the smoke out to sea.

weird but true!

The Santa Ana winds can carry a single spark for miles.

In Australia, wildfires are called bushfires. The word "bush" refers to Australia's wilderness areas.

Australia also has many wildfires because it is hot and dry. In parts of Australia, global winds called El Niño (el NEEN-yoh) can cause the weather to be hotter and drier than usual. This helps fires spread.

On the Move

During a wildfire, animals need to protect themselves. Small animals, such as frogs and turtles, burrow underground. Others hide under rocks or in nearby logs until the smoke and flames have passed. Many run or fly to safety.

For quick creatures such as bobcats, a fire is a great time to grab a snack. They try to catch animals escaping the fire.

A white stork feeds on insects escaping a wildfire. Firefighters sometimes see bugs and other small animals flying or running out of the forest just ahead of the flames.

Bugs That Love Fire

While many animals avoid wildfires, the fire beetle looks for them. The beetle's body has special sensors that help it find the heat in a burning forest. The bug searches for trees that are still smoldering and lays its eggs in and under the bark. The young beetles inside the eggs grow. After they hatch, they use the tree for food.

In addition to fire beetles, charcoal beetles and jewel beetles also seek out fires.

fire beetle

Hot Word

SMOLDER: to burn slowly with smoke but no flame

On the Bright Side

After a fire, sunlight can shine on a forest floor, allowing new plants to grow.

Although wildfires can cause a lot of damage, they are also an important part of some ecosystems. Some forests can get so crowded with young trees that not much sunlight reaches the forest floor. This makes it hard for other plants to survive. Fires can thin out these crowded forests so that tall trees, seedlings, and wildflowers can grow.

Wildfires also help forests by burning dead leaves and plants on the ground. The ashes add nutrients to the soil, which helps plants grow. In addition, fires can remove sick plants and insects that kill trees.

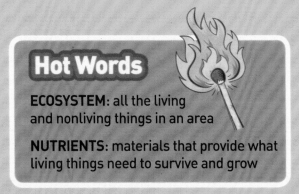

Hot Words

ECOSYSTEM: all the living and nonliving things in an area

NUTRIENTS: materials that provide what living things need to survive and grow

Wildfires help forests in another way, too. Some evergreen trees do not release their seeds without the extreme heat of a forest fire!

During a fire, heat rises to even the highest tree branches. The heat melts the waxy coating on the tree's cones. Now the cones can open and drop their seeds to the ground. After the fire, new trees can sprout in the soil.

closed

open

Rocky Mountain lodgepole pinecones

New pine trees begin to grow in this burned forest in the Rocky Mountains, U.S.A.

A prescribed burn is not a wildfire because it does not burn out of control. Firefighters start these fires and make sure they stay only in certain areas.

Scientists did not always understand how important wildfires are. Firefighters used to put out every wildfire, large and small. But now we know that many forests need fires to stay healthy. Some fires are allowed to burn if they are not a danger to nearby property.

Hot Word

PRESCRIBED BURN: a fire that is set on purpose to help an ecosystem

Sometimes fires are set on purpose to help an ecosystem. Fire managers work with firefighters to protect and help forests. They decide when an area needs a prescribed burn. Prescribed burns also remove some fuel from an area. This helps prevent extreme wildfires.

6 COOL FACTS About Wildfires

Up to 100,000 wildfires start around the world each year.

1

The flames of a forest fire can reach 1472° Fahrenheit.

2

The black-backed woodpecker makes its home in burned forests.

3

4

Wildfires can cause hurricane-force winds.

5

Firefighters often name wildfires based on the animals, woods, or water sources in the area.

6

Four out of five wildfires are caused by humans.

Wildfire Warriors

Some wildfires become so dangerous that they need to be stopped. Specially trained people called wildland firefighters quickly spring into action.

Hot Word

FIRE LINE: a line of cleared and dug-up land made by firefighters to control a fire

Wildland firefighters work together to dig a fire line around a fire.

These firefighters often clear away brush and dig a long ditch to create a fire line. They remove the fuel the fire needs to move and grow. When the fire reaches the fire line, it goes out because it has no more fuel to burn.

Hot shot crews are a special group of firefighters in the United States. They work in groups of 20 to battle the toughest parts of fires. They can be called on anytime, day or night. They are sometimes even sent around the world to help fight wildfires.

Hot shot crews are among the most skilled firefighters in the United States. To keep in shape for fighting fires, they often train all year long.

Smoke jumpers have to carry a lot of their gear with them when they parachute to the ground.

Fire Tornadoes

When winds kick up during a fire, air may spin so quickly that it forms a long, swirling funnel called a fire tornado. These funnels of flames start and end quickly. Though they whirl like a tornado, they are different from the tornadoes that form during storms.

Smoke jumpers are another group of highly trained firefighters. They parachute into fire zones from planes. They get to the scene quickly and then fight the fire on the ground.

weird but true!

The center of a fire tornado can reach 2000° Fahrenheit.

A helicopter drops water on a fire.

Sky Jell-O is colored pink so that it can be seen easily.

For the largest fires, firefighters may get help from the air. Planes can drop thousands of gallons of water on a fire at a time. They also drop a pink fire retardant that some people call "sky Jell-O." This material coats areas that have not yet burned, making it harder for those fuels to catch fire.

Hot Word

FIRE RETARDANT: a material that can slow or stop the spread of a fire

Mark Thiessen

Photographer Mark Thiessen is also a firefighter. He has worked alongside other firefighters for up to 16 hours at a time. Thiessen has even driven through raging forest fires to get his stunning photos, like the one below.

Tools of the Trade

Firefighters use lots of special tools to battle wildfires.

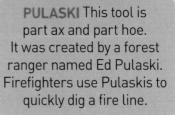

PULASKI This tool is part ax and part hoe. It was created by a forest ranger named Ed Pulaski. Firefighters use Pulaskis to quickly dig a fire line.

CLOTHING A wildland firefighter's clothing is made of lightweight material that can be in temperatures up to about 700° Fahrenheit without burning.

GEAR PACK A gear pack can weigh 30 to 50 pounds. It holds food and water for the firefighter, as well as an emergency shelter and flares.

PELLETS Firefighters call these small white pellets "Ping-Pong balls." When the balls are dropped from helicopters, chemicals inside make them ignite. Sometimes they are used to burn out fuel between a fire and a fire line. This helps stop the fire.

TRUCK A wildland fire truck is built to drive on rough ground. It can carry up to five firefighters and at least 500 gallons of water to remote areas.

Fires in Focus

All around the world, large wildfires are remembered for the damage they cause.

UNITED STATES In 1871 the Peshtigo Fire burned 3.8 million acres in Wisconsin and Michigan, killing 1,500 people.

SOUTH AFRICA In 2008 one of Africa's biggest natural wildfires burned more than 200,000 acres of forests in South Africa. The fires swept through villages, destroying homes and killing more than 45 people.

RUSSIA In 2003, 157 fires burned more than 27 million acres of land in Russia's Siberian forests. The area was so large, information had to be gathered by satellite.

AUSTRALIA The Black Friday Bushfire of 1939 burned 5 million acres of land. Ash from the fires even rained over New Zealand, 2,000 miles away.

After the Fire

A forest is a busy place after a wildfire. New plants begin to grow. The soil is rich with nutrients, and more sunlight reaches the ground. This helps the new plants grow quickly.

Fires do not always burn a whole forest. Sometimes only small sections burn. Other times, trees can survive the flames. If a fire burns along the ground, the tops of trees may not be harmed.

When plants return to a forest, animals are not far behind. New flowers bring insects, birds, and other animals. The animals use the plants for food. They also help spread the plants' seeds. This helps the forest grow back even faster.

Many animals make their homes in trees after a fire. Birds make nests. Insects live in the bark. The forest quickly becomes full of life again.

Safe and Sound

Learning about wildfires helps us protect nature and ourselves. At fire science labs, scientists learn as much as possible about fires. Their work helps us understand wildfires and how to battle them safely.

Scientists at fire science labs study how smoke affects the air we breathe, how fires spread, and how fires affect plants and animals. They learn more about the chemicals used to put out fires. They also help create new tools to fight fires. The more we know about wildfires, the better we will be at keeping people safe.

Scientists at the Missoula Fire Sciences Laboratory in Montana, U.S.A., use a wind tunnel to study how fire behaves.

Not all fires can be stopped from happening, but many can. Here's what you can do to help.

✓ Do not start campfires during dry spells.

✓ Build campfires only in fire pits.

✓ Do not build a campfire without the help of an adult.

✓ Never leave a campfire unattended.

✓ Put out a campfire completely before leaving or going to sleep.

✓ Call 911 if you notice a fire that is out of control or unattended.

Smokey Bear

Since 1944, Smokey Bear has been an important symbol of preventing wildfires. His message, "Only you can prevent wildfires," reminds people that careless actions can cause fires.

Remember - Only you can
PREVENT FOREST FIRES

ONLY
YOU
CAN PREVENT
WILDFIRES.

Ad Council
SMOKEYBEAR.COM

SMOKEY

Smokey Bear got a makeover for his 70th birthday in 2014. He is also now active on Facebook and Twitter.

QUIZ WHIZ

How much do you know about wildfires? After reading this book, probably a lot! Take this quiz and find out.
Answers are at the bottom of page 45.

Which of these is not part of a fire triangle?

A. heat
B. fuel
C. water
D. oxygen

Which animal looks for wildfires instead of avoiding them?

A. fox
B. fire beetle
C. ant
D. deer

Which type of fire burns in the tops of trees?

A. surface fire
B. crown fire
C. ground fire
D. spot fire

What kind of firefighters parachute into fire zones?

4

A. hot shot crews
B. smoke jumpers
C. fire line diggers
D. sky Jell-O droppers

What helps new plants grow quickly after a fire?

5

A. The soil is rich with nutrients.
B. There is often more rain.
C. There is less sunlight.
D. The tops of trees may not be harmed.

6

What is Smokey Bear's fire safety message?

A. Firefighters are your friends.
B. Only you can prevent wildfires.
C. Stay away from fires.
D. Fires can start anywhere.

How can you help keep wildfires from starting?

7

A. Never leave a campfire unattended.
B. Put out a campfire completely before leaving.
C. Do not build a campfire without the help of an adult.
D. all of the above

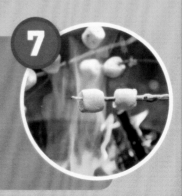

Glossary

CROWN: the top part of a tree

FIRE RETARDANT: a material that can slow or stop the spread of a fire

FUEL: any material that can be burned to produce heat or power

OXYGEN: a colorless, odorless gas that is in the air we breathe

PRESCRIBED BURN: a fire that is set on purpose to help an ecosystem

ECOSYSTEM: all the living and nonliving things in an area

FIRE LINE: a line of cleared and dug-up land made by firefighters to control a fire

IGNITE: to catch fire

NUTRIENTS: materials that provide what living things need to survive and grow

SMOLDER: to burn slowly with smoke but no flame

WILDFIRE: an uncontrolled fire that occurs outdoors, especially over a wooded area

Index

Boldface indicates illustrations.